LE PAPILLON

as recorded in *Enchanting Versailles*

Strictly Classical

Piano

Claude BOLLING

2

3

4

9

CLAUDE BOLLING

LE PAPILLON

for Alto Saxophone and Piano

HAL•LEONARD®
CORPORATION

7777 W. BLUEMOUND RD. P.O. BOX 13819 MILWAUKEE, WI 53213

LE PAPILLON

as recorded in *Enchanting Versailles*

Strictly Classical

Saxophone alto

Claude BOLLING

4

6

7

© 1994 CAÏD

8

12

14

20

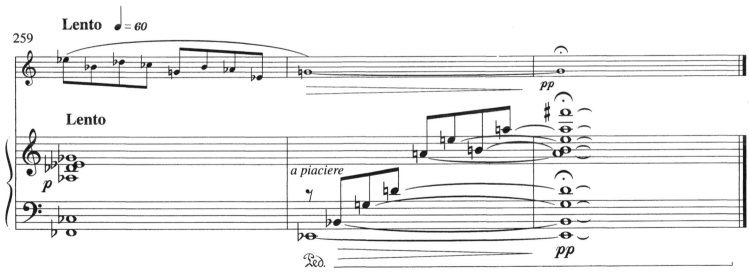